Endorsements for the Church Questions Series

"Christians are pressed by very real questions. How does Scripture structure a church, order worship, organize ministry, and define biblical leadership? Those are just examples of the questions that are answered clearly, carefully, and winsomely in this new series from 9Marks. I am so thankful for this ministry and for its incredibly healthy and hopeful influence in so many faithful churches. I eagerly commend this series."

R. Albert Mohler Jr., President, The Southern
Baptist Theological Seminary

"Sincere questions deserve thoughtful answers. If you're not sure where to start in answering these questions, let this series serve as a diving board into the pool. These minibooks are winsomely to-the-point and great to read together with one friend or one hundred friends."

Gloria Furman, author, *Missional Motherhood*
and *The Pastor's Wife*

T0326847

"As a pastor, I get asked lots of questions. I'm approached by unbelievers seeking to understand the gospel, new believers unsure about next steps, and maturing believers wanting help answering questions from their Christian family, friends, neighbors, or coworkers. It's in these moments that I wish I had a book to give them that was brief, answered their questions, and pointed them in the right direction for further study. Church Questions is a series that provides just that. Each booklet tackles one question in a biblical, brief, and practical manner. The series may be called Church Questions, but it could be called 'Church Answers.' I intend to pick these up by the dozens and give them away regularly. You should too."

Juan R. Sanchez, Senior Pastor, High Pointe Baptist Church, Austin, Texas

"Where can we Christians find reliable answers to our common questions about life together at church—without having to plow through long, expensive books? The Church Questions booklets meet our need with answers that are biblical, thoughtful, and practical. For pastors, this series will prove a trustworthy resource for guiding church members toward deeper wisdom and stronger unity."

Ray Ortlund, President, Renewal Ministries

What Is the Church's Mission?

Church Questions

What Is
the Church's
Mission?

Jonathan Leeman

:: CROSSWAY®

WHEATON, ILLINOIS

Trade paperback ISBN: 978-1-4335-7855-7
ePub ISBN: 978-1-4335-7858-8
PDF ISBN: 978-1-4335-7856-4
Mobipocket ISBN: 978-1-4335-7857-1

Library of Congress Cataloging-in-Publication Data

Names: Leeman, Jonathan, 1973- author.
Title: What is the church's mission? / Jonathan Leeman.
Description: Wheaton, Illinois : Crossway, 2022. | Series: Church questions Includes bibliographical references and index.
Identifiers: LCCN 2021048689 (print) | LCCN 2021048690 (ebook) | ISBN 9781433578557 (trade paperback) | ISBN 9781433578564 (pdf) | ISBN 9781433578571 (mobipocket) | ISBN 9781433578588 (epub)
Subjects: LCSH: Mission of the church.
Classification: LCC BV601.8 .L435 2022 (print) | LCC BV601.8 (ebook) | DDC 266--dc23/eng/20220128
LC record available at https://lccn.loc.gov/2021048689
LC ebook record available at https://lccn.loc.gov/2021048690

Crossway is a publishing ministry of Good News Publishers.

BP		31	30	29	28	27	26	25	24	23	22
15	14	13	12	11	10	9	8	7	6	5	4	3	2	1

And Jesus came and said to them, "All authority in heaven and on earth has been given to me. Go therefore and make disciples of all nations, baptizing them in the name of the Father and of the Son and of the Holy Spirit, teaching them to observe all that I have commanded you. And behold, I am with you always, to the end of the age."

Matthew 28:18–20

Does a book on the church's mission sound, well, a little abstract or academic? Maybe not that relevant to your day-to-day Christianity?

I'd like to suggest it's very relevant, especially in seasons of growing political and cultural turmoil.

When people feel the pressures of political division or cultural decline, that's all they want to talk about. They'll post on social media, "Now is the time to take a stand and fight." As I'm writing this, Christians on the political right declare this in response to LGBTQ+ revolutionaries and threats to religious freedom. Christians on the left say the same about racism and structural injustice. And how many Christians decided to take their stands in response to COVID-19 quarantines, masks, or vaccines?

Yet that sense of urgency is worth paying attention to no matter where you are or when you live as you consider the topic of the church's mission. The church's mission is what Jesus calls the church to do, but our convictions about what he calls us to do are often shaped not just by him but by the political or economic challenges we're feeling. Those realities feel most urgent. So, if as a Christian you're able to open your Bible and find anything at all remotely connected to those challenges, you'll be tempted to shape the mission of the church around them.

Do you feel oppressed? The Bible opposes oppression. So you could say the church exists to oppose oppression.

Do you worry about the decline of morality in your nation? The Bible opposes the decline of morality in a nation. So you could say the church exists to fight for a moral nation.

Do you care about good government? The poor? Material blessing? Finding purpose for your life? Healthy families? The Bible addresses all of those things. So you could say the church exists primarily for those things. At least that will be your temptation.

I know pastors who, twenty years ago, said it wasn't in their job description to tell people how to vote or to lead marches. In recent years that has changed. They say unprecedented times call for unprecedented measures. Circumstances changed their sense of urgency.

No doubt, there are times to take stands or do the unusual. Yet it's precisely in these moments we need to be especially careful, lest our churches veer off track. The temptation to swerve grows when strife grows. More than anything, then, days of cultural turmoil and political tumult require us to double down in studying Scripture.

How Will You Spend Your Weekdays and Weekends?

More broadly, differing views of the church's mission lead to different ways of thinking about the Christian life. Start with your weekdays. Is it better to go into vocational ministry? If not, how should you view your job in relation to your Christianity?

Think about your evenings and Saturdays. Should you prioritize getting to know your neighbors? Sharing the gospel? Volunteering in a homeless shelter? Getting more involved politically?

As for your Sundays, what should a church do when it gathers—teach Christians to share the gospel or to fight structural injustices? And what kind of work should we do together—sponsor missions trips or soup kitchens?

These kinds of questions can weigh on Christian consciences, and we can feel guilty about not doing enough. Sure, Jesus calls people to give up everything and follow him. But what does that mean practically?

Mind you, the conversation about the church's mission is bigger than deciding how to spend your time this coming week. It includes all of life and the universe, things present and things to come, even heaven and hell. If hell really exists, and if unrepentant people really are going there, and if it's really your church's job to warn them, then you and I need to reckon with that fact pretty quickly.

Really, you should care about the church's mission because, as a Christian, you don't want to worry about the wrong things but to instead devote your life to the right things, the weighty things.

What Kind of Church Will You Join?

The conversation about the church's mission also impacts what kind of church you will join. Different churches will shape your conscience, your spiritual life, and your worship differently. What your church counts as "normal, faithful Christianity," you will soon count as "normal, faithful Christianity." Spend a few years in a church where the preacher and the members emphasize topic X, and you will most likely soon emphasize topic X. If they talk about Y, you'll talk about Y.

One of your most important spiritual goals in life, therefore, should be to place yourself and your family in a church whose mission reflects the teaching and burdens of Scripture.

Yet look closely. I can point you to four churches that post the same statements of faith on their websites. But walk into these four churches on a Sunday morning, or look at their budgets, or watch their pastors' social media feeds, and you'll discover these churches follow different playbooks.

Church #1 emphasizes the Great Commission and Jesus's command to make disciples. Yet when they say "make disciples" they mean "make converts." So Church #1 gears everything in the church toward non-Christians, as if local churches basically exist for the sake of evangelism. They talk about Christian growth some, but their programs focus on individuals, not the corporate body or family. They don't see the connection between their evangelism and being a vibrant, united, other-worldly family. Based on Church #1's mission playbook, let's call it *Seekers Church*.

Church #2 is similar to Church #1 (Seekers Church), but it appeals less to middle-class longings for things like purpose and more to basic human desires for health and wealth. Join their service on Sunday, and you'll hear about God's desire to bless us, if only we would have enough faith. Based on its playbook, let's call Church #2 *Prosperity Church.*

While Churches #1 and #2 emphasize how Jesus is here for us, Churches #3 and #4 emphasize how we are here for Jesus. Church #3 we can call *Justice Church.* Join them on Sunday, and you'll hear the preacher say we should care for the downtrodden, wake up to the nation's structural injustices, attend to the environment, and generally do good in the world.

Church #4 is another version of Church #3, but it focuses on the structural injustices that concern political conservatives, like abortion, same-sex marriage, and religious freedom. Call it *Righteous Nation Church.* It wants to save the nation from moral decay and make it safe for Christianity.

At best, both Justice Church and Righteous Nation Church focus on discipleship, the moral shape of Christians, and the command to love our neighbors. At worst, they risk sliding a foot, or at least a toe, into Phariseeism, meaning, they lay down laws and political certainties where Scripture doesn't. Members leave church on Sunday not so much thanking God for his grace in their lives but feeling superior to other people because of their moral and political convictions.

To be sure, many churches occupy a couple of these examples. I'm simply outlining stock types, not trying to caricature your church, so that we can all be more careful.

Furthermore, I trust that some variety between churches is God given. Just like an individual Christian working on Wall Street and one teaching in a rundown school will have different daily ministries, so a church in the suburbs might have a strong counseling ministry while a church next door to a refugee camp might excel in serving the poor. Praise God!

Still, there's a difference between *being sensitive* to the economic waves and political winds surrounding us and *being driven* by those waves and winds. When churches are driven, their playbooks—their sense of their mission—easily succumb to biblical imbalances and worldly agendas. Seekers Church shows signs of having succumbed to consumerism, Prosperity Church to materialism, Justice Church to political progressivism, and Righteous Nation Church to nationalism, even if all four have orthodox statements of faith.

If you're from another time or place than I am, you might have different stock types to offer. That's fine. Describe what you see. But you get the point: when we're talking about the mission of the church, it's easy to let our sometimes good, sometimes bad temporal concerns write the church's playbook. We risk giving such things an outsized importance, or giving these things the wrong job, or even making them an idol. This might sound strange, but a church can actually promote things affirmed by the Bible and still be driven by a worldly agenda.

To return to my earlier point, then, deciding which church to join is one of the most important spiritual decisions you can make because your church can shape you, by varying degrees, with a worldly agenda or a biblical one. In turn, you will give your evenings and weekends, your work and your family, to better or worse purposes.

Making Disciples, Being Disciples

Let me describe a fifth church, one that offers the church playbook commended in this book. I'll call it *Disciples Church*. Like Seekers Church, Disciples Church says our mission roots in the Great Commission—"Make disciples." Yet folks in Justice Church and Righteous Nation Church will be glad to hear that following just behind, like a train car attached to the locomotive, is the Great Commandment—"Love God and love your neighbor." After all, the Great Commission commands us to "make disciples," but it also commands us to "observe everything [Jesus] commands."

Join Disciple Church's weekly gathering, and you'll hear the bad news about our sin and God's judgment, but then you'll hear the good news about Jesus Christ dying and rising again as a payment for and to free us from sin. With this news in mind, this church then works to "make disciples." A disciple is a follower of Jesus.

"Making disciples" doesn't just include evangelism or helping people to become Christians. It includes helping people to grow as Christians. Think about it. "Making" a tree house or a cake or anything involves both starting the task and finishing it. You don't say you "made" a cake and point to a bowl of unbaked batter. Likewise, Jesus's command to make disciples includes both baptizing people into the faith *and* teaching them to obey everything he commanded. It involves the whole Christian life—from infancy to maturity.

Therefore, Disciples Church gathers every week to help people follow Jesus, as Paul says, "until we all attain to the unity of the faith and of the knowledge of the Son of God, to mature manhood, to the measure of the stature of the fullness of Christ" (Eph. 4:13).

Yet Disciples Church also captures and emphasizes something the other four too often miss: the fact that the Christian life is corporate. When we're born again, we're born again into a family (see 1 Pet. 2:10). Maturity is defined by "unity of the faith," as we just saw. Practically, says Paul, this means "the whole body, joined and held together by every joint with which it is equipped, when each part is working properly, makes the body grow so that it builds itself up in love" (Eph. 4:16). A tough sentence to follow, but the gist is, maturity involves the whole body building itself up in love.

This is crucial for a conversation about the mission of the church because it means we now have two jobs to think about: the job of the whole family and the job of every individual member of the family—an "our" job and a "your" job. Jesus has assigned certain duties to the whole family for when we act together as a family, and he has assigned other duties for each of us as individual members acting separately. It's the whole family's job, for instance, to build up the family, but it's your job to love your kids and go to work and greet your neighbors.

Failing to recognize this distinction leads to lots of misunderstanding on the topic of the mission of the church. If you ask one Christian friend, "What's the mission of the church?" he might answer with the whole church in mind and give you an "our" job answer. If you ask another, she'll answer with the individual members in mind and offer a "your" job answer. Yet we need both answers, each for its part.

What is the mission of the church according to Disciples Church?

- Acting all together as a church, our mission is to *make disciples*. That's the whole family job.
- Living as individual church members throughout the week, our mission is to *be disciples*. That's the job of each individual family member all week.

Or picture two circles: a bigger circle called "being disciples," and inside of that a smaller circle called "making disciples." Your life mission as a church member is everything contained in that bigger circle of being a disciple. Yet when you come together to act as a whole church, your distinct mission together is to make disciples.

You might think of the relationship between a law school and a lawyer, or medical school and a doctor. The law school and medical school circle have one job (making lawyers and doctors), while lawyers and doctors themselves have another job (being lawyers and doctors).

An even better illustration, which I'll unpack later, is the relationship between embassy and ambassador. Our churches are embassies, and each one of us is an ambassador.

The Disciple-Making Dimension in Being a Disciple

Let me make one more connection between these two ways of talking about the church's mission before getting to the argument itself. *Making disciples* plays a central role in *being* a disciple. It's not as if a church member can say, "I don't need to worry about making disciples. That's just a job for the whole church or the church leaders." No. It's a central part of being a disciple.

Look again at the previous illustration of the two circles, but now picture it as a solar system. That larger circle, which represents the Christian discipleship as a whole, is like the orbit of a planet. The smaller circle, which represents our gatherings as local churches and the work we do all together, is like the sun. First, it illumines, shining its light into our lives so that we can see them more clearly ("I thought I was being a pretty good husband, but as I listen to the sermon I realize there's some serious room for improvement!"). Second, it creates a gravitational pull on our whole lives, giving all of life a "disciple-making" dimension.

I prepare breakfast for my children. Why? Because I want them to eat, yes, but also because I want them to experience the heavenly Father's love for them. I want them to be disciples.

I attend staff meeting and listen to reports that don't naturally interest me, but I work hard to listen. Why? Because I will be able to better do my job, yes, but also because I want to model Christ's love for all people. I want them to grow as disciples.

I want to install a shower next to the spare bedroom in my home's basement. Why? So guests in our home can conveniently shower without coming upstairs, yes, but also because I want our home to be a comfortable place of hospitality, pointing to Christ's own provision for us. I want all our guests to become or to grow in discipleship.

You could extend these illustrations into every area of your life: raising children, doing art, planting a garden, playing sports, engaging politically, taking vacations. As a Christian, you are united to Christ, and everything you do represents Christ. Therefore, everything you do has a disciple-making dimension. Indeed, the highest and best way to love our neighbors is to point them to God. Augustine said that love of mother or brother, friend or fellow worker, spouse or stranger, is no love at all unless it's given with respect to Christ.[1]

Furthermore, it's the weekly work of the whole church which creates this gravitational pull on the rest of our week. The gathering, together with the work of the church, enables and equips us to enter the rest of our weeks *being* disciples and with disciple-*making* mindsets. To be sure, we won't spend every second of every day thinking about making disciples. We think about raising our children ("Did my wife say I pick them up from school today?"), going to work ("I hope I do a good job on this work proposal"), and getting the car fixed ("Why does the steering wheel keep pulling left?"). Yet we pursue all these activities, to some extent, with *making disciples* in mind. We want our children, our colleagues, our mechanic, even our enemies to know Christ. And we want our fellow church members to know Christ more.

After all, nothing is better and more joy-giving in life than knowing Christ, and knowing Christ in everything we do and everywhere we go.

Yet so far I've just been asserting my conclusions. I've yet to make the argument. Is this what the Bible really teaches and prioritizes? In order to help you understand why the Disciples Church prioritizes making disciples in its playbook, as well as why I divided the church's mission into *making disciples* and *being disciples*, we need to ask three questions.

Question 1: What Is Humanity's Biggest Problem?

This first question is one I learned to ask in discussions like these from my friend Sebastian, a business entrepreneur and former fellow elder. During complicated elder meeting conversations, he would bring our meandering discussions back into focus by asking, "What's the problem we're trying to solve here?"[2]

Likewise, when a church comes to think about its mission, it needs to ask itself, what's the biggest problem we're trying to solve here?

Seekers Church uses the language of sin, but it frames the idea of sin in a *consumeristic* and *therapeutic* way. As if you're sitting on a psychologist's couch, the preacher appeals to how you're *feeling* and *what you want*. Your sin is that little bit of selfishness that keeps you from being the dad or mom, friend or neighbor, that you really want to be. It's your unbelief in God's love for you. Seekers Church says Jesus will help you solve these problems.

Prosperity Church, too, uses the language of sin, but its emphasis is *material*. Your sin is your lack of faith, which acts like a clog in the pipe through which God's material blessings could flow. The effects of God's curse—scarcity and death—are the problems to solve, more than the transgression and guilt which led to the curse, at least judging by the airtime given to each.

Justice Church and Righteous Nation Church also use the language of sin, but the emphasis is *ethical*. Like a parent or a judge, their preachers appeal to how you're *living*. The more progressive Justice Church talks about the injustices we see in things like poverty, inadequate housing, failing schools, an ailing environment, racism, and what it calls structural injustices. Meanwhile, the more conservative Righteous Nation Church talks different structural injustices, even if it doesn't call them that: divorce law, gay marriage, hindrances to religious freedom, media bias, abortion, the LGBTQ+ agenda in public schools, and more.

Finally, Disciples Church doesn't deny the therapeutic, material, or ethical aspects of our lives. It wants you to discover God's purpose for your life, to enjoy his good material gifts, and to live justly and righteously. It simply knows that, when such concerns take center stage, we have probably succumbed to consumerism, materialism, or some variety of moralism, respectively.

When Disciples Church talks about sin, its emphasis is *theological*. Sin is first and foremost an offense against God. God has said, "I'm your Creator and King." Yet from Adam onward we have lived as if we were our own creators and kings. We have broken his law and sought our own glory instead of his (Rom. 3:23). Therefore, he has declared us guilty and promised eternal death (Rom. 6:23; Rev. 20:11–15). Our biggest problem is not the LGBTQ+ political steamroller (as folks on the political right will say) or racism (as folks on the left will say), though both of those are significant problems. Our guilt before God and his wrath against it, by far, is the biggest problem to solve.

Distinguishing Root Problems and Fruit Problems

That said, Disciples Church doesn't ignore all the personal sins and structural injustices that Justice Church and Righteous Nation Church oppose. The Bible points a sad, trembling finger at both the quiet disobedience of Adam as well as the public wickedness of Pharaoh. It pronounces woe against the sexually immoral as well as "those who decree iniquitous decrees" (Isa. 10:1; Est. 3:7–14), sins intentional and unintentional (see Leviticus 4), transgressions individual and national (see Isaiah 13–19). It indicts personal partialities against the poor (James 2:1–7) and works to fix structural inequalities that divide ethnicities (Acts 6:1).

Yet Disciples Church distinguishes between root problems and fruit problems, causes and symptoms. Our sin against God (singular "sin") is our root problem. Our sins against others (plural "sins"), whether personal or structural, are the fruit problem that follows. In fact, Disciples Church has the firmest basis to call everything from racism to abortion to the ideologies of this world unjust precisely by insisting that these practices and structures are fundamentally opposed to God (Ps. 51:4). When a man gets beaten and robbed, the good Samaritan should care about him because he's made in *God's* image (see Luke 10:25–37). When a brother or sister is poorly clothed and lacking in daily food, the Christian shouldn't say, "Go, I wish you well; keep warm and well fed," because he or she is made in *God's* image (see James 2:16). Apart from God, evil doesn't exist.

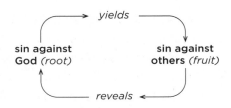

Nothing outweighs our defiance of God's law and our denigration of his glory. God is the weighty one, the consequential one, the eternal one, the law-giving one, the just one, and the one by whom all reality and righteousness are measured.

The Significance of Hell

One way to comprehend the weight and significance of our sin against God and his glory is to meditate on the horror and eternality of hell. No doubt, the idea of hell is tough. It's emotionally unsettling in the extreme. But I want you to stare at it for a second and not just wish it away. If hell does exist, we don't do anyone a favor by wishing it away.

A question to think about is, why does Jesus, again and again, offer such sobering images of hell, as when he talks about "undying worms" and "unquenchable fire" (e.g., Mark 9:48)? That's pretty vivid language, Jesus.

The reasons are (1) because hell really is that bad, whether such language is metaphorical or not, and (2) because the terror of these images convey how terrible sin is and—by inverse proportion—how weighty and glorious God is.[3] After all, wrath reveals worth.

My siblings and I discovered at a young age, for instance, that lying to our parents yielded a stronger penalty than bickering about a toy. Why? The truth is worth more than toys. The more precious the reality, the more terrible the consequences. Every jewelry store owner will tell you the same.

It's the very eternity and awfulness of hell, in other words, that shows us how really, really bad sin is and, therefore, how really, really good and worthy God is. Sin dulls our senses, shrinks our horizons, and anesthetizes us to reality. Sin tells us we're the center of the universe and that God *owes* us. The Bible's descriptions of hell wake us up to a much bigger, grander universe, like moving from a stick-figure world on paper to the real world. Life is more precious, the stakes higher, God's glory greater than you ever imagined.

Let's summarize the answer to question 1. What is humanity's biggest problem? It's our sin against this holy, just, and glorious God, whose infinite nature and divine being are more precious than all the universe, even as the potter is far more precious than the pot he fashions. Growing out of our sin against God, we sin against others. A church, therefore, should keep its eyes on both the root problem and the fruit problem and always make sure to give proper weight to each.

Question 2: What Is the Solution to Our Biggest Problem?

Churches #1 through #5 all talk about biblical things like forgiveness, good works, and God's blessings. Yet it's possible to give genuine biblical goods an outsized importance or the wrong job. We want good works, but to give good works the job of saving the neighborhood or nation is damning. We want the blessings of health and wealth, but to treat them as guaranteed promises for this world creates false expectations and risks making them idols.

If we want to give biblical things the right job and emphasis, we need to make sure we're reading the Bible's whole storyline. Understanding the storyline rightly helps us understand the Bible's news of a solution rightly. You take this for granted when reading news. You know that if a reporter gets the news story wrong, he'll get the news headline wrong.

Therefore, Disciples Church does its level-best to read every part of the Bible. Here's one way to summarize each part:

Created to image God	Genesis 1–2: God makes people in his image and gives them a world to fill and subdue forever, so long as we do so in obedience to him, thereby "imaging" his love, holiness, and glory.
Putting ourselves in the place of God	Genesis 3–11: We forsake God and God's blessings by casting off his rule and working for our own glory, earning the curse of death.

Repeating the lessons: image God, but they don't	Genesis 12 through Israel's history: God employs a people, Israel, in order to teach the lessons of Genesis 1–3 over a thousand years and on an international stage. He gives them Adam's original task: image or display God's holiness, love, and glory for the sake of blessing the nations. He even gives them his law and presence to help. Yet Israel repeats Adam's error, and so God casts them out like he did Adam.
God must do it	The Prophets: The prophets present the Old Testament's takeaway lesson: God himself must provide the solution. He must come, pay for sin, and change our hearts. He must conform us to his image and enable us to obey his law so that we can display his holiness and love and glory and receive all his blessings.
Jesus saves	The Gospels: Jesus Christ is God's coming. He came as God to win a people for himself by solving our guilt problem through dying and rising again. And he came as man to do what Adam and Israel didn't: image God's holiness and love and receive all the promised blessings of God.

| The Spirit unites us to Christ and gathers us as the family of God and embassies of heaven. | Acts through Revelation: Christ's Spirit unites us to Christ, so that what Christ is, we are: forgiven, righteous, and tasked with displaying God's holiness and love. He also gathers us together as the family of God and embassies of heaven. Together we anticipate the day when Christ comes again and remakes everything completely. |

That's a quick summary of the storyline. What is the news headline that captures all of it? The news headline is what the Bible calls the "gospel," which is a word that simply means *good news*.

What is the gospel? Think through that storyline again. We can discern three newsworthy items that comprise the gospel, including a change of status, a new family, and the promise of more to come. First, the gospel includes a new covenantal status, just like a person gains a new status when he marries (see Hos. 2:16–23; 1 Pet. 2:10). Being united to Christ means we're declared forgiven and righteous because of what he did in his life, death, and resurrection. God made him who knew no sin to be sin, so that we might become the righteousness of God (2 Cor. 5:21). Christ paid the penalty that we deserved through his death on the cross, rose from the dead indicating that he defeated sin and death, and won all the promises of God promised to Adam, Israel, and David (see also Rom. 5:8–9; Gal. 4:1–7; 1 Cor. 15:1–5; 2 Cor. 2:3).

Second, the gospel includes a new covenantal family (Eph. 2; 1 Pet. 2:10). Our conversion is corporate. Being adopted by the heavenly Father means getting a whole bunch of brothers and sisters to boot.

Third, the gospel includes a new covenant promise of our sanctification and perfection as well as the remaking of the whole universe (e.g., Rom. 8:21, 30; 1 John 3:2; Rev. 21). Christ has replaced our hearts of stone with hearts of flesh so that we want to obey God's law (Jer. 31:31–34; Ezek. 36:24–27). And one day, we will obey him perfectly, a day in which heaven and earth themselves will be remade and all things made right.

All this is *news*. It refers to something God has *done* and promises *to do*, not to something we *must do*. We cannot solve our sin problem. We cannot recreate our hearts, the city, the culture, or the cosmos. We can only point to the one who does these things: God the Father, God the Son, and God the Holy Spirit.

Rejoice, Christian! God has forgiven your sin and declared you righteous. He has united you to a new family. And even now he's conforming you to his image, with the promise that one day he will perfect you completely, even as he remakes the universe completely.

Change Happens

Yet there's a human counterpart to *what God does* in providing our gospel solution: *what he calls and empowers us to do*. Flowing out of God's gospel will be our God-given gospel obedience. We cannot repeat Christ's unique work of being a sin-covering, substitutionary sacrifice, by which we are justified. Yet beyond that he calls us to do what he has done. "As the Father has sent me, even so I am sending you," Jesus says (John 20:21).

Remember what we saw in the storyline above. The goal all along was for Adam and Eve to fill and subdue the earth and to do so in a way that images or displays the holiness and love and glory of God. Therefore, it's not enough to say, "Jesus did it." We also have to say, "Now we do likewise." Doing this doesn't save or justify us, but it's what God-saved and God-justified people do.

Remarkably, Christ gives us his Spirit for these purposes. When God's Spirit causes a person to be born again, change happens. Always. A newborn baby cannot help but breathe and cry and eat and act according to its nature. Likewise, a newborn Christian, someone who has been recreated by God's own Spirit, cannot help but love God, God's law, and God's people.

Maybe you remember this from when you became a Christian. Before becoming a Christian, you wanted to indulge certain sins. Yet after, you didn't. Maybe you loved getting drunk. Then you didn't. Maybe you enjoyed taking advantage of people. Then you didn't. Maybe you despised Christians. Then you found yourself loving them.

Maybe you had no interest in God's book. Then you found yourself fascinated by it. I'm not saying the desire for all sins vanished, but I am saying a change began. And you could feel the change.

Reborn people love righteousness. Justified people pursue justice. Those forgiven of sin fight sin, personal and public. And members of Christ's heavenly body attach themselves to an earthly body, where together we "put on" and "clothe" ourselves with these God-given, new-creation, born-again, heaven-on-earth realities (Col. 3:1–17).

We could draw the two-part solution as a flow chart: God's gospel work creates the gospel obedience of a gospel people, and our gospel obedience as a gospel people in turn manifests, displays, and proves God's gospel work, like this:

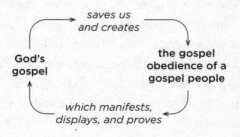

saves us and creates

God's gospel

the gospel obedience of a gospel people

which manifests, displays, and proves

We don't do any of this perfectly. Far from it. We are like newborn babes who learn to crawl, then walk, and then run only gradually. Plus, our old natures remain mixed with our new natures for now (Romans 7). But little by little, in fits and starts, from one degree to the next, God's love is perfected in us. The apostle John writes, "And by this we know that we have come to know him, if we keep his commandments. Whoever says 'I know him' but does not keep his commandments is a liar, and the truth is not in him, but whoever keeps his word, in him truly the love of God is perfected" (1 John 2:3–5).

I recall how one friend changed when he became a Christian. Before Christ, he was marked by laziness, selfishness, and the pursuit of cheap pleasures. After becoming a Christian, he became a different person—one marked by a tender concern for others and self-control. He began studying the Bible daily and invested more and more in his church. After several years of this, he even became an elder in the church. Everyone who knows him today would characterize him as deeply compassionate, hard-working, and holy.

Christians cannot take credit for such new desires. Sometimes quickly, sometimes slowly, they show up. The Spirit of God gives them, particularly as we expose ourselves to his word and his people.

We Cannot Bring Heaven to Earth

That said, the Spirit does limit his work, at least at this moment between Christ's first and second comings. He regenerates our hearts, minds, ambitions, desires, and loves. But he does not regenerate our hands or the work of our hands. Bodies still die. Houses still crumble. Foundations still sink. Good governments turn bad. Beautiful songs are forgotten. Even the best preachers can say untrue things. In a word, the curse remains in full effect, and will until Christ comes again. Christ may rule over every square inch of creation, but so does the curse. Read Ecclesiastes. Everything "under the sun" is still futile and "meaningless," says the inspired author (1:1–7). The wise die just like the foolish (Eccles. 2:16). The place of justice produces injustice (3:16). And an honest day's work will kill you (10:8–9).

Because of this, you should be leery of anyone who says the mission of the church is to "redeem the culture" or "transform the city." Yes, each of us as Christians should work to leave our little section of the garden better than we found it. We try to make a dent. We seek to do good. Indeed, we're commanded to do good (Gal. 6:1). But we do this for the sake of faithfulness, in accordance with our new nature. We don't do it because we can "redeem" or "transform" anything. Such language confuses whose job is whose. The Holy Spirit has the work of redeeming and transforming, not us, and the kingdom of heaven goes no further than God's life-giving Spirit.

To put it another way, we cannot bring heaven to earth, whether in our politics, our social work, our construction projects, or any of our good deeds.

That said . . . God can.

But God Can

The gospel does redeem a culture and transform a city. It's not the city listed on your driver's license. It's the heavenly city of God. Your local church becomes an outpost or embassy of it. We cannot bring heaven to earth now. But God can.

Sometimes God does make his dwelling with us *now*. Heaven comes to earth. So God walked with Adam and Eve in the garden, meaning heaven and earth overlapped there. He dwelled with Israel in the temple, meaning heaven touched down on earth there too (see Ex. 34 and Heb. 9:23).

Most perfectly and prominently, God dwelled on earth through Jesus Christ. Jesus, in his own person, was the kingdom of heaven on earth (see Matt. 4:17).

Yet there is one more place that heaven touches down on earth even now, and that's in the local church. Heaven shows up most prominently in our gatherings (see Heb. 12:22). There we bind and loose "on earth" what's bound and loosed "in heaven" (Matt. 18:18). There the one with all authority in heaven and on earth dwells (Matt. 18:20; 28:18). Paul therefore calls the church the temple of the Spirit (1 Cor. 3:17; 2 Cor. 6:16).

In other words, central to the work of a church is showing the world what heaven is like. We represent heaven, like embassies. In your gathered congregation and mine, the world should encounter the first fruits of a heavenly culture, city, and even language. There we learn to live in meekness and mercy, purity and poverty of heart, peace-making and hungering for righteousness (Matt. 5:3–10). There we practice speaking with love, joy, peace, patience, kindness, goodness, faithfulness, gentleness, and self-control (Gal. 5:22–23). There we demonstrate the power and Spirit of heaven in our hearts (1 Cor. 12:4–10). There the non-Christian should enter and say, "God really is among you!" (see 1 Cor. 14:25).

Your local church is an outpost or embassy of the kingdom of heaven. And you are an ambassador of it (see 1 Cor. 10:31; 2 Cor. 5:20). Remember what I said about Seeker Church failing to recognize the connection between evangelism and the growth of the body? God intends to hold his people up as a display of his glory before the nations. Churches should therefore take membership seriously. They need to make the line between the church and the world bright and clear, as clear as the line between clean and unclean or holy and unholy among God's Old Testament people. We do this through a careful and disciplined approach to baptism and the Lord's Supper.

What's the gospel solution to humanity's biggest problem? One way to summarize everything we've discussed so far is to say that the answer is God. God is the solution. The solution is not merely escaping hell. Turn your gaze from hell to heaven and behold God! God is more wonderful and weightier than hell is terrible and eternal. He is almighty, infinite, everywhere, perfect, and good. He is self-sufficient and the Creator of everything that exists, even time and space. He is holy. He is love. He is the greatest good, the greatest joy, the source of all love, and the only true satisfaction of our souls. As Augustine famously observed, "Our hearts find no peace until they rest in you."[4]

Therefore, directing people's hearts and minds to God is the most important thing a church can do and the singular activity around which everything else revolves. We do it with our words and deeds.

Yet pointing to God also means pointing to God's people, the assemblies of God's people, and the call to obedience among God's people. Inside our local assemblies we practice and work at being a new society, a new culture, a holy nation, even heaven on earth. We show the nations what it's like to dwell with God.

Question 3: What Is the Church's Mission?

We are back to where we began. What do the answers to questions 1 and 2 mean for the church's mission?

If humanity's problem comes in two parts (a root and fruit problem), as does the solution (God's gospel and gospel obedience), so does the mission: all together churches should prioritize *making disciples*; separately, individual members should focus on *being disciples* (which includes making disciples).

Priority 1: Go and Make Disciples . . .

Jesus's final words to his disciples before ascending into heaven were, "Go therefore and make disciples of all nations . . ." (Matt. 28:18).

What's involved in making a disciple? First, we have to "go." Every church and church member should be interested in the gospel's spread across political and ethnic boundaries—to "all nations"—either by going or supporting those who do.

More broadly, going to make disciples means thinking about evangelism and conversion. This is the entry point to everything else. The Seeker Church gets this exactly right. Conversion addresses the root problem and places us on the pathway for addressing the fruit problems. At conversion, people's hearts change. Their confidence, trust, and worship change. Even the goal of their good works changes—from self-glorifying to God-glorifying.

Apart from conversion, everything else is ultimately for naught. You can solve pollution and global warming, stop abortion, resolve all racial inequity, end global hunger, provide refuge for every victim of abuse and trafficking, negotiate peace treaties, and indeed, gain the whole world. And, all things being equal, a full stomach is better than an empty one (but see Hos. 13:6). Yet Jesus might still reply, "What will it profit a man if he gains the whole world and forfeits his soul" (Matt. 16:26)?

Satan offered Jesus this very bargain. He took Jesus "to a very high mountain and showed him all the kingdoms of the world and their glory. And he said to him, 'All these I will give you, if you will fall down and worship me'" (Matt. 4:8–9). Jesus could have had it all then and there: rule over all the kingdoms of the world. He could have passed whatever laws he wanted on the contested political issues of his day or our day. He could have outlawed all abortion, dramatically improved every criminal justice system, and established empire-wide schools in which no child was left behind. Yet how right, pure, and durable would all these structural changes have proved with a compromised worship at its heart?

The point here is not about putting the soul before the body. It's about putting the eternal before the temporal and worshiping the one who can throw both soul and body into hell (Matt. 10:28). We will rightly care about secondary things only when we keep them secondary. People might criticize Christians who prioritize evangelism and conversion with being "so heavenly minded they're no earthly good." But in fact, the most heavenly minded person does the most earthly good. He knows his treasures are stored up in heaven, leaving him free to sacrifice his treasures here for the good of others. Or as John Piper explains, "Christians care about all suffering, but especially eternal suffering."[5]

... By Baptizing and Teaching

Yet conversion involves more than a one-time event—a crossing from death to life. Listen to the rest of Jesus's command where he tells us how to make disciples: "Go therefore and make disciples of all nations, baptizing them in the name of the Father and of the Son and of the Holy Spirit, teaching them to observe all that I have commanded you" (Matt. 28:19–20).

We make disciples *by* baptizing and teaching. Specifically, churches baptize people "into the name" of Father, Son, and Spirit. Baptism gives people the Jesus "name tag" or "team jersey." It identifies individuals with Christ and Christ's people. Churches baptize, at least in part, so that Christians can begin to "gather in [the] name" of Christ with other believers (Matt. 18:20). As such, churches ordinarily baptize new converts into church membership (see Acts 2:41). Exceptions exist, as when missionaries go to places churches don't exist (see Acts 8:38). Yet ordinarily baptism makes a church responsible for an individual's discipleship, saying, "She's with our Lord and us," while the new believer says, "I'm with the Lord and them."

If baptism is the front door into church membership, the Lord's Supper is the ongoing family meal. The Supper is not a private matter. It reveals and displays who the body of Christ on earth is (1 Cor. 10:17).

Remember what I said earlier about what local churches are: embassies of the kingdom of heaven. An embassy is a useful illustration because it calls attention both to how churches represent another kingdom as well as how they possess a formal authority that individual church members don't possess: the keys of the kingdom (Matt. 18:18–20; cf. 16:19). The keys allow churches to declare who belongs to the kingdom of heaven and who does not, which they do through baptism and the Supper (or the withholding of the Supper in discipline). You might think of an embassy for your country in another part of the world. If you're living in that part of the world, the embassy doesn't have the authority to make you a citizen, but it can identify you as a citizen by renewing your passport. To join a church, likewise, is to be formally recognized by other Christians as a fellow citizen and ambassador of a heavenly kingdom.

Once a new disciple has been recognized by a church, the disciple submits him or herself to job training. We must learn how to be citizens and ambassadors for this kingdom. To that end, a church will teach its members to observe everything Jesus commanded. Churches teach through preaching, singing, praying, and reading the Bible. Elders teach in word and deed (Acts 20:26–30; 1 Tim. 4:16; Heb. 13:7, 17). Yet every member also teaches by modelling Christlikeness for one another and speaking the truth in love to one another so that the body builds itself up (1 Cor. 11:1; Eph. 4:15–16, 29; see also, 1 Thess. 1:6–7; 2 Thess. 3:7; Heb. 13:7). Teaching for a changed life is what the Justice Church and Righteous Nation church rightly emphasize.

What's helpful to realize in all of this is, a body of Christians growing up together in righteousness and love in turn serves the purposes of evangelism—Seeker Church's burden. Jesus promises that, as we learn to love each other inside the church with his own forgiving and forbearing love, the world will know what he's like (John 13:34–35). Elsewhere he says that our good works will lead people to praise God (Matt. 5:16; also, 1 Pet. 2:12). In short, evangelism creates a marked-off and holy people, and that marked-off and holy people in turn serves the purposes of evangelism by providing an attractive witness.

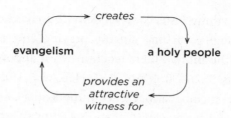

To put it another way, local churches are the means and ends of the Great Commission. They exist to make disciples.

Priority 2: Being Disciples by Observing Everything Jesus Commands

Yet our discussion of the church's mission cannot stop just yet. After all, Christ calls us not just to make disciples, but "to observe everything I have commanded you" (Matt. 28:20).

Using myself as an illustration, Jesus intends for me to observe everything he's commanded as a church member and church elder, yes, but also as a father to my daughters, a husband to my wife, a child to my parents, a citizen, a writer, a seminary professor, a neighbor, a friend, a car driver, a homeowner, a grocery shopper, a restaurant patron, a utilities customer, and on and on.

Let's pick one of those examples: restaurant patron. The whole church doesn't go with me into the restaurant. The whole church's job is not to tip my server. The whole church's work, remember, was to identify me with Jesus through baptism and the Supper. It named me as a Jesus ambassador. Yet now there I sit in the restaurant booth, trying to decide how much to tip my server. And my individual decision about a tip will represent Jesus well or poorly. So it is in every other domain of my life because my church has formally declared me to be a Jesus ambassador.

Notice, then, we need to talk about two different jobs: the embassy job of the whole church and the ambassadorial job of every member. Which is why we need to talk about the church's mission in two different respects—the whole church's mission and the individual member's mission. The mission of the embassy and ambassador are highly related and interdependent, but they remain distinct, like law school and lawyer are distinct.

Sometimes people disagree about the mission of the church because they have different answers to questions 1 and 2 about humanity's greatest problem and the solution to that problem. Liberal Christianity, for instance, often treats our greatest problem as ignorance and the solution as education. Put those two answers together and you'll then conclude the church's mission is to educate. Among people who share the same evangelical theology, disagreements can also result in using the word "church" differently. Sometimes people mean the organized or gathered local church when they talk about the church's mission. This includes things like decisions about membership and discipline, a church's budget, pastors' job descriptions, matters discussed in a church business meeting, and certainly what a church does during its weekly worship gatherings. And sometimes people have the everyday and scattered church in mind— church members as they go about their week.

So if someone starts talking to you about the mission of the church, you should ask them, are you talking about what God asks our whole congregation to do *all together*? Or are you talking about what he asks each member to do *indi-*

vidually? Part of the problem here is that many Christians have not been taught to think of their faith in corporate or family terms. They think in terms of "me" not "we," even when they're talking about the church.

As I said earlier, *our* mission as a local church acting together is to *make disciples*, while *your* mission as an individual church member is to *be a disciple*.

Our mission: If I'm standing in front of my entire congregation, and I'm addressing their collective work together, I will say, "Our mission as a church acting all together is to *make disciples*. We are to organize our gatherings, install pastors, think through any additional programming, use our budget, and send each other out at the end of every church service in pursuit of the work of making disciples. The organized and gathered local church is like an embassy. Our task is to make official declarations on behalf of the kingdom of heaven: 'This is the gospel' and 'These people are gospel citizens.'"

Your mission: But then I'm also going to exhort them as individuals and explain what their job is going into their week: "Your mission as a representative and agent of this body is to *be a disciple*." Meaning: live your life, love your family, go to work, be a neighbor, gather with the church, and scatter to care for the world around you both for the purpose of making disciples and for showing the world what heaven is like in everything you do. Your words and deeds together represent King Jesus.

	Our mission **acting all together**	Your mission **everywhere**
Summary	Make disciples	Be a disciple
Bible text:	". . . baptizing and teaching them . . ."	. . . to observe everything I commanded." (Matt. 28:19)
Illustration	Embassy	Ambassador

Both Hats Required

We need churches doing the work of churches and church members doing the work of church members, and every Christian wears both hats at different times.

You personally will have a different amount of formal authority or "say" in your church, depending on whether your church has a congregational, presbyterian, or episcopalian governing structure. And the preacher will certainly have the loudest voice. But you as a member participate in that ministry by your presence, your giving, and every other ministry you undertake in the life of the congregation. You are all moving in the same direction, so that "the whole body, joined and held together by every joint with which it is equipped, when each part is working properly, makes the body grow so that it builds itself up in love" (Eph. 4:16).

The priority you place on making disciples in turn creates a gravitational pull on the rest of your life, both so that you live as a disciple and so that you always have disciple-making in mind.

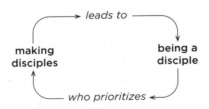

A final illustration: I remember when my four children were little. I can assure you that my wife, who was at home all day with them, did not prioritize in a day-to-day sense evangelizing our neighbors, though she tried as she could. She prioritized just getting through the day with the children safe and fed—while keeping her sanity! Yet in a larger sense, yes, she wants more than anything for our four girls to know Christ, and for her mothering to in turn be a witness to our neighbors. Both of us parent ultimately to that end. We love our daughters by caring for their persons. Of course. But we love them most of all by pointing them to Christ. And belonging to a church helps us to do both kinds of work, each for its part.

What's the mission of the whole church? Making disciples. What's the mission of every member? Being disciples who prioritize making disciples, so that the nations might discover the pleasure of knowing God, becoming like him, and displaying his glory (Matt. 5:16; Eph. 3:10; 2 Pet. 1:3–4; Rev. 7:9–12).

Notes

1. Augustine, *On Christian Doctrine*, trans. D. W. Robertson (Indianapolis: The Bobbs-Merrill Company, 1958), 3.10.16; 1.23.
2. Personal stories involving other individuals are shared in this booklet with permission. Often pseudonyms have been used for privacy.
3. This paragraph and the next two have been updated and adapted from my contribution to Ed Sexton (ed.), *Four Views of the Church's Mission* (Grand Rapids: Zondervan, 2017).
4. Augustine, *Confessions*, trans. R. S. Pine-Coffin (New York: Penguin, 1961), 21.
5. John Piper has used this phrase in numerous sermons and articles. You can find it used throughout his resources available at DesiringGod.org.

Scripture Index